African Metalwork

CW00735840

Cover: Forest Scene, Yekinni Folorunsho

Contents

Foreword

A wealth of African art has existed in Britain for over a hundred years, held in museums such as the British Museum and the Horniman Museum in London and the Pitt Rivers Museum in the University of Oxford. Brought out of Africa by government officials, missionaries, anthropologists and collectors, this art was for long seen as having curiosity value rather than aesthetic merit, but increasingly artists have turned to these collections as a source of imagery and inspiration.

Among the rich traditions of African art to be found in these collections are works of the goldsmiths and brass casters of Asante. Many of these Asante works were brought to Britain in 1896 (the year before the infamous 'punitive expedition' against Benin) when the British invaded the Asante kingdom, entering the capital Kumasi, exiling the young king and ransacking his palace. Among the material they brought back were three bronze or brass jugs or ewers that were different in style and form from Asante work. It turned out that these were of English manufacture and had been made around 1390 for the court of Richard II. How or when they arrived in Kumasi no-one can say with any certainty, but what they illustrate is the way in which cultures intertwine, like strands in a rope, separate but linked.

The art that was brought back to Europe from Africa around the turn of the century was to have a crucial influence on modern artists in the West, notably Derain,

Goldweight, Ian Auld Collection

Vlaminck, Picasso and Matisse, among many others. Painting and sculpture in the first decades of this century were radically changed by this new aesthetic, this new way of seeing the world.

This exhibition sets out to explore one aspect of African art and craft, looking at the use of metal. Starting with the brasses of Benin and the gold paraphernalia (brass goldweights, gold-dust boxes etc.) of the Asante, and following this up to the present day with a range of objects for domestic and ceremonial use. Work from leading contemporary metalworkers, including forged iron furniture from the Jua Kali Metalwork Guild of Kenya, is shown, together with objects sold in the markets of Africa: pots, pans, kitchen utensils, suitcases, milk churns.

The Crafts Council is most grateful to Magdalene Odundo for the work she has put into creating this exhibition, and to Yvonne Ayo for her invaluable research support on the project. The exhibition also owes a debt to the research work of Chris Russell, and to the help of our panel of advisors, Nigel Barley of the Museum of Mankind, Anthony Shelton of Brighton Museum and Art Gallery, John Picton of the School of Oriental and African Studies, University of London and the metalworker and independent technical advisor Dr. David Poston. Our thanks for valuable advice also go to Keith Nicklin of the Horniman Museum, John Mack of the Museum of Mankind, Elspeth Court of the School of Oriental and African Studies, and Wanjiku Nyachae. Jeremy Coote of the Pitt Rivers Museum and Ian Fowler receive particular thanks for their generous advice and support in the latter stages of the project.

The Crafts Council and Magdalene Odundo would like to extend warm thanks to the many people in Africa without whose help this exhibition could not have happened. They cannot all be thanked by name, but special mention must be made of Nike Davies of the Nike Centre for Art and Culture, Oshogbo, Nigeria, Alan Donovan and Charles Ndibe of African Heritage, Nairobi, Wendy Goldblatt of the Crafts Council of South Africa, Deo Kafwa and Patrick Injamana of Nyumba Ya Sanaa, Dar Es Salaam, Tanzania, Mr Kasugga, Uganda, and Gonzaga Consultants, Nairobi.

Finally, our thanks go to the many makers throughout Africa whose work is shown in this exhibition and without whose assistance this exhibition could not have been brought together.

Jacqueline Ford
Head of Exhibitions

5

Traditions of Transformation:

An Introduction to the art of African Metalwork

Jeremy Coote

Blacksmith forging hoe blade,
Azorsapliga, Ghana

Right and this Page: Goldweights,
Ian Auld Collection

Overleaf: Heating clay moulds to melt out
wax original. Natunia, Ghana.

8

Introduction

Just last week I was told about the work
of Siedou Ouattara, a blacksmith working
near Bondoukou, Côte d'Ivoire. Ouattara
learned his craft in Numuso, the blacksmiths'
quarter of Soko, but is now based in
Motiamo. He uses old cars as a source
of material, using different parts for making
different types of objects: the springs for
making traps, the chassis for making hoes,
and the wheel-rims for making the
clapperless bells that are used to announce
the arrival of the chief and to accompany
the dancing of the shrine-priest. Ouattara
is just one of thousands of metalworkers
working in Africa today and one of what

must be hundreds of thousands of Africans
who have worked metal at some time in
history. Ouattara is an African metalworker,
but in what sense can he be said to be
contributing to a tradition of African
metalwork? He is clearly contributing to the
maintenance and development of local
metalworking traditions, but what
relationship does his work have to other
African traditions, to those of Benin brass-
casters, Akan goldsmiths and Yoruba
blacksmiths, for example, or more distantly
to those of metalworkers on the other side
of the continent, to those of the silver-
workers of Ethiopia or of the royal smiths
of Karagwe in north-western Tanzania?
Arguably, Ouattara's work has little to do
with any of these traditions and far more
in common with the work of blacksmiths
in small urban centres in other developing
countries, not only in the rest of Africa,
but throughout the world.

The continent of Africa is vast, roughly three
times the size of Europe, with an ancient
and complex history. Its terrain varies from
the deserts of the Sahara and the Namib,
through savannah grasslands and scrub,
to rainforests. More than a thousand
different languages are spoken in Africa
and its populations live in hundreds of
thousands of different communities in
a variety of environments – from isolated
rural settlements, through villages and small
towns to major urban conurbations like
Nairobi, Lagos and other contemporary
African cities. Today, the continent comprises
more than fifty nation states whose borders

only minimally reflect the spheres of influence of the hundreds of nations and kingdoms of pre-colonial times. Most of these communities, both today and in the past, have had metalworking or at least metal-using traditions. Where communities were geographically or culturally related, regional traditions may be said to have existed, but even the most expansive of these never spread across the whole continent.

Moreover, Africa has never been insulated from the outside world. In fact many of its peoples have participated in inter-continental traditions. For example, from early times people, and their ideas and material culture, have gone back and forth between North Africa and the rest of the Mediterranean and between East Africa (including Madagascar) and the Arabian Gulf and Asia, and in more recent times between everywhere on the continent and Europe and, perhaps most significantly, in very large numbers between West and Central Africa and the Americas. It is difficult, therefore, to talk about *the* tradition of African metalwork, rather there are hundreds if not thousands of traditions. Nor are they confined to the continent itself. For example, transformed versions of Yoruba and Kongo religious traditions, involving the use of iron figures and ritual objects, flourish in the Americas, especially in Brazil and Haiti, but also in new manifestations of old cults in New York and other urban centres with large African American populations. African metal-workers based in Britain, as well as black

British metalworkers of African origin, also continue to contribute to African traditions. The work of the London-based Kalabari artist Sokari Douglas Camp is well known, but there are many other British-based artists whose work continues and transforms African traditions as well as, through exhibitions and publications, feeding back into work being done today in Africa.

History
Historically, the metals used the most in Sub-Saharan Africa were iron, copper, the copper-tin alloy bronze, the copper-zinc alloy brass, and gold, but there has also been some localized use of lead, tin, silver and, recently, aluminium. There are substantial deposits of alluvial and reef gold in Africa, as well as substantial amounts of haematite, magnetite, limonite and other iron ores. While copper is sparse in West Africa, it is plentiful in parts of Central and Southern Africa. It is not

Removing mould containing molten metal from furnace using a hooked stick. Natunia, Ghana

known when native metals were first worked, but from the archaeological record we know that, in parts of Niger and Mauritania at least, copper was being smelted by the early first millennium BC. Our knowledge of African metallurgical history at this time and for the next 2000 years is sketchy (though, thanks to assiduous work by archaeologists, growing all the time), but it seems that by AD1000 only the Batua and San peoples of Central and Southern Africa lacked knowledge of metal, while elsewhere in the continent its use was virtually universal. By this time also there were established trade networks across the Sahara by which gold was taken north, often being exchanged for the more valued brass, while less extensive local trade routes had probably been in existence for centuries.

For decades scholars have argued about the origins of metalwork traditions south of the Sahara. For most African metalworkers, such arguments are irrelevant, knowledge of metalworking having been given to the first smith by a god or ancestor. The major impetus to Western historical thinking about such questions was provided by the influx into Europe of hundreds of Benin 'bronzes' (in fact, brasses) after the sacking of the City of Benin by a British Punitive Expedition in 1897, and by the later archaeological discoveries at Igbo-Ukwu, Ife and other Nigerian sites. In the early years of this century many scholars could not believe that black Africans had invented for themselves the complex

technical processes used to produce these objects, while more recently some have tried to argue that the limited evidence available justifies theories that techniques such as these were developed independently south of the Sahara. Today it seems that the most reasonable assumption to make is that metalworking technology spread southwards from North Africa, where metalworkers had for long drawn on the traditions of the rest of the Mediterranean. What most confused scholars in the past, and must be stressed here, is that the sequence of Ages – Stone, Bronze, Iron – which is such an embedded part of Western thinking in these matters, does not apply to the history of metal in Africa. Rather, almost everywhere iron and copper (and the copper alloys bronze and brass) were introduced at about the same time.

Metal has had many important roles to play in African history. In raw, processed and worked forms it has been a major item of exchange, contributing to the opening up and maintenance of trade routes within and beyond the continent. Gold was a major factor in the creation and maintenance of Trans-Saharan trade routes, and brass – and later iron – were major items in the trade between the European powers and the kingdoms of West Africa from the late fifteenth century on. Over the centuries, major transformations were brought about with the export to the continent of vast quantities of metal from Europe. As early as the sixteenth century, for example, at what was coincidentally

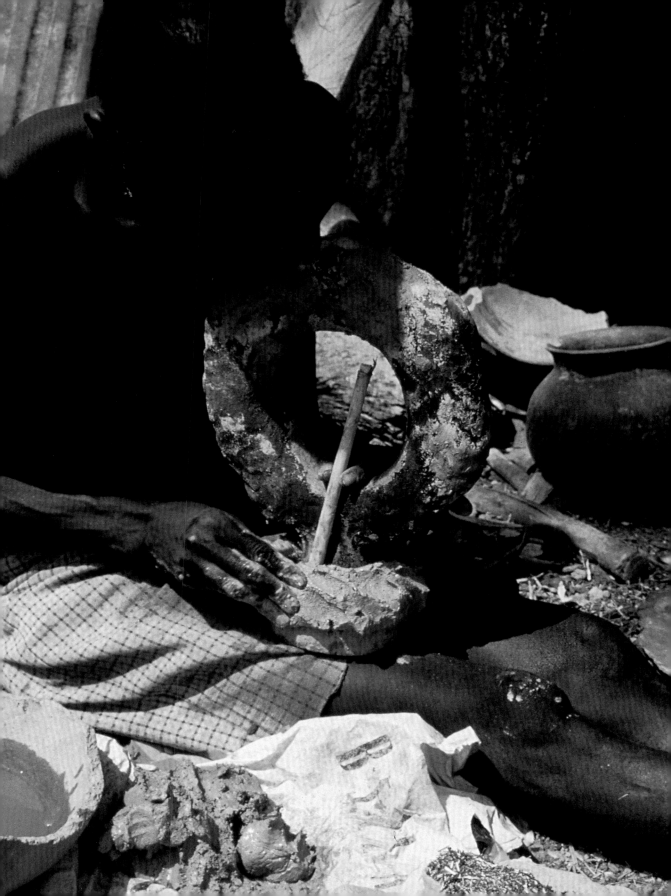

Attaching crucible containing scrap brass to mould using fresh clay. Polmolgo-Sirigue, Ghana.

Overleaf: Contemporary male ancestral shrines outside compound entrance, commonly containing metal artefacts relating to occupation of deceased. Zoko, Ghana.

a period of rich artistic development in Benin, the Portúguese brought large quantities of brass manillas (metal currency bars) to the kingdom. These were melted down and used by Benin brass-casters to produce great numbers of the figurative plaques and other objects that have become universal symbols of African culture and civilization. In many areas the import of iron gradually led to the abandonment of local smelting and to the loss of local smelting knowledge; in such areas the smith today is often a repairer rather than a maker of objects. It also led to the tying of local economies into wider capitalist systems and to the loss of economic independence. Metal continues to be imported into Africa in large quantities, not least in the form of cars and other machinery that eventually provide Ouattara and other smiths with the resource out of which to meet the local demand for metal objects.

Metalworkers

Generally, African metalworkers have belonged to separate groups within the wider society, and this continues to be the pattern in many areas. In centralized kingdoms like Benin, for example, metal-workers, like other craftspeople, were organized into guilds. The separateness of African metalworking groups does, however, take other distinctive forms. This is especially so of blacksmiths, groups of whom maintain their separateness by following a rule of endogamy, that is, only allowing members to marry within the group; characteristically, the wives of smiths are potters. This separateness may be physically manifested, with smiths and their families often living at the edges of settlements, on the margins between the village and the bush or forest.

Such blacksmithing groups take a number of forms. The Awka of south-eastern Nigeria, for example, are itinerant craftsmen who work metal for a number of different peoples. Among the Mande peoples of Mali and neighbouring countries, smiths comprise separate hereditary groups, often described as 'castes' in the literature. Among the Tuareg, Maasai and other nomadic and semi-nomadic peoples, smiths tend to be ethnically distinct, with no members of the dominant ethnicity practising the art. The social status of the smith is generally an ambiguous one. His position in the local society tends to be marginal and the attitude of others towards him a mixture of contempt, fear and respect. Frequently, the smith also has the role of circumciser, burier of the dead and charm- or amulet-maker. In West Africa in particular, for example among the Bamana and Dogon of Mali, the smith is often a wood sculptor too, producing masks and figures for masking societies and local religious groups. In contrast, in Western Equatorial Africa and around the lakes of East Central Africa there are strong associations between smithing and political authority with, in some societies, smithing being an occupation of kings.

Any attempt to understand the position of the smith, and other metalworkers, in African societies must start with his technical ability to turn raw materials into useful and beautiful objects. The metalworkers' skills probably seem as extraordinary to non-smiths in Africa as they do to non-smiths everywhere else. But in Africa it is not just a matter of the smith's technical abilities, it is also a matter of his ability to use his knowledge of medicine and ritual to invoke and control supernatural forces. During his apprenticeship a smith not only learns the technical skills necessary for dealing with varying raw materials and their behaviour under different atmospheric conditions, but also how to make offerings and sacrifices to the spirits and ancestors. He also learns how to protect his work against malevolent spirits and magic, in part through placing substances in or around the smelting furnace. Commonly it is also vital for the smith to abstain from sexual intercourse during the smelting process and for fertile women – locally conceived as either all women between the menarche and the menopause, or menstruating women only – to keep away. The complex meanings underlying these practices may be illustrated by the fact that metallurgy is conceived of as a sexual activity in much of the continent. In places as far apart as Niger and Zimbabwe a furnace is said to be a woman who gestates iron and gives birth to a bloom.

Art Forms

African metalworkers have created a stunning array of forms for every conceivable type of object. Like other African objects, the products of metalworkers are often not what they might at first appear to be, their superficial form not always indicating their main purpose. For example, stylized hoe-blades were used as a form of currency, for bridewealth in marriage exchanges, throughout much of Central Africa. Metal weapons have been used to hunt and to fight, but also as ceremonial objects and status symbols. Some of the distinctive throwing-knives produced in Africa were made for use, many more are impractical as weapons. Moreover, they were often important cultural items among peoples living in heavily forested areas where their practical utility would have been extremely limited. Items of metal jewellery have been used to adorn and beautify the body, but also function as a way of storing wealth and of marking status. Similarly, items of metal regalia and insignia are objects of adornment, but more importantly symbols of political and social status. Metal musical instruments have been used to entertain, but also as a means for communicating with ancestors and spirits, while metal sculptures and masks have also been made to entertain, but more importantly used to make manifest, or aid in communicating with, the ancestors and spirits. Finally, some items have less immediately obvious functions. Yoruba iron staffs adorned with figures of birds are used to ward off witchcraft.

This page: Gold weight,
Ian Auld Collection.

Overleaf: Blacksmith selling
hoe blades. Bolgatanga
Market, Ghana.

One who follows the track of the elephant never gets wet from the dew on the bushes

Metal forms frequently differ little from the same forms made in wood or some other material. At least, they differ little superficially. Clearly, the aesthetic qualities of a metal object are different. It is likely to be heavier and to reflect light in a different way. More importantly, however, metal objects carry different meanings. Often, metal is rare or expensive to obtain and thus highly valued, while the difficulty of working it adds to the value of the object and thus to the status of the owner. Such qualities of metal are more or less universal, and not specific to Africa. What is more distinctive is the way in which different metals are associated with gods and their powers. In Benin, for example, brass and ivory continue to be regarded as the most enduring materials and therefore those most suitable for royal art. They are *the* symbols of permanence in Benin thought. For the people of Benin, all metal has inherent power derived from Ogun, the god of metal, but brass in particular has the power to avert evil forces as it is both red in colour and very shiny. Among the Yoruba, Ogun is the god of war and iron and is honoured with iron objects. These range from miniature smithing tools to ceremonial swords and staffs as well as amulets and other emblems. Shrines with iron objects are erected to him by his vast range of iron-using devotees both in West Africa and the Americas, including blacksmiths, hunters, warriors, barbers and, in recent times, mechanics and lorry-drivers.

Probably the major African contribution to the metalwork of the world is in the medium of lost-wax casting (sometimes known by its French name *cire perdue*). It is this technique that was used to produce many of the most famous of African metalworks, namely the brasses and bronzes of Igbo-Ukwu, Ife and Benin in Nigeria, and the goldweights of the Asante and other Akan-speaking peoples of Ghana and Côte d'Ivoire. The material recovered from archaeological sites at Igbo-Ukwu is dated to the end of the first millennium AD and comprises a range of elaborately decorated vessels, 'altar stands', bowls, pendants, staff ornaments and so on. More famous are the cast brass and cast copper heads, masks and figures from Ife, dated to the twelfth to fifteenth centuries. More famous still are the Benin 'bronzes' (in fact brasses) that were produced from about the fourteenth century onwards. Many of them are virtuoso pieces, Benin casters using elaborate systems of armatures and runners to enable them to produce complex free-standing figures,

Soldering silver candlestick.
Niamey, Niger.

various ceremonial objects and the high-relief plaques that adorned the palace walls.

Almost as famous, and as technically sophisticated, are the detailed, miniature brass goldweights produced by casters among the Asante. These were used for weighing the gold dust used at one time for all commercial transactions, more than half a million of them being produced from the sixteenth century or so. They are generally classified into two types, geometric (or abstract) and figurative. The former comprise squares, crosses, cubes, discs, pyramids and so on, decorated with a variety of patterns. The tradition of abstract designs may have been adopted from the Islamic peoples to the north, from whom a part at least of the Asante weighing system was adopted, but any symbolism that these designs may once have had is now lost. The latter feature a variety of manmade objects as well as human and animal figures. A few of the weights illustrate proverbs, which are a central feature of Akan life and culture, while the majority feature proverbial objects and can thus be associated with a number of different proverbs. Thus, for example, a weight representing a leopard and an elephant may illustrate a particular, in this case unknown, proverb. Each creature, however, features in a number of proverbs, for example 'One who follows the track of the elephant never gets wet from the dew on the bushes' (meaning 'Follow an important man and he will protect you in time of trouble') and

'When the rain falls on the leopard it wets the spots on the skin but does not wash them off' (meaning 'A man's nature is not changed by circumstance').

Conclusion

Africa is too vast and diverse for there to be a single tradition of African metalwork. A broader perspective, however, allows us to appreciate both the rich and complex history in which African metalwork has participated and that, both in and out of Africa, African metalwork continues to thrive. The mounting of exhibitions such as *African Metalwork* helps to bring the various traditions, both historical and contemporary, together. Through exhibitions and catalogues such as these, African artists in and out of Africa will have opportunities to draw on what they see has been done elsewhere. The variety, richness and diversity of Africa and its cultural traditions will ensure that no single style results, but that exciting new traditions will emerge, to be the subject of other exhibitions, here or elsewhere, in the future.

Jeremy Coote
Oxford, 1995

I should like to thank Karel Arnaut for telling me about the work of Siedou Ouattara.

Magdalene Odundo
talks to Linda Theophilus

Masqueraders, (detail) Yekinni Folorunsho.

Magdalene, you have been researching and selecting this exhibition over the past two years. What were your initial aims for the exhibition?

When **africa95** was first conceived, at a first meeting, my interest in it was the opportunity to consider African metalwork as a whole. Other art forms have been shown in this country, including textiles, pottery and, of course, traditional sculpture. I wanted to look at metalwork – in terms of aesthetic values, as well as functional and utilitarian values. Classical and historical African metalwork is well known; jewellery and body adornment has also been written about and exhibited, and its regard as an exotic item, worn by the exotic peoples of Africa, has not been doubted.

In this exhibition I have tried to present, to a British audience, a more complete picture. My aim is to show that historical and contemporary work can be viewed as a continuum; that, as in fine art through-out the world, classical and historical work can, and does, inform the contemporary, while the contemporary re-interprets, and moves on.

During the initial stages of **africa95**, Susan Vogel (who curated the exhibition *Africa Explores* at the Liverpool Tate) suggested the possibility of touring the festival exhibitions in Africa, as well as in Britain. This was a very interesting prospect for me – it would have meant bringing the work 'home', to revitalize interest and awareness

Edan, Ian Auld Collection.

Overleaf: Goldweights,
Ian Auld Collection.

in it. In my experience traditional jewellery, for example, had been taken for granted among my parents' generation, and, by some of my generation, considered 'pagan' and 'primitive', not 'chic' like a necklace of Coca-Cola bottle tops.

It would have been an opportunity to develop a reappraisal of the art of metalwork by present-day youth, and to extend its teaching and practice in mainstream education. I would have liked to create a dialogue among Africans, to access and reassess the importance of the role of art, through the art of metalwork – in some areas metalwork is traditionally considered of higher status than, say, pottery.

Although, sadly, an African tour may not be possible, these aims have also shaped the research and informed my selection.

It was always recognized that this one show could not represent the whole of Africa. How did you select the countries that you have focused on?

Once I recognized that we could not include work from all the countries, or even all the regions, I decided to have sections covering not countries but work for different purposes – ceremony, body adornment, domestic metalwork and tools, and weaponry, and to incorporate both historical and contemporary work in each section. For practical and financial reasons, we also had to restrict ourselves to Anglophone countries – and still it was

not possible to visit all of these.

The antiquities of Ghana and Nigeria – Asante gold, Benin brasses – are known in Britain, through items in public and private collections. However, contemporary work from these countries has not been collected to any extent and much will be new to the British viewer – for example Ghanaian and Nigerian work in the exhibition includes silver filigree jewellery by Benjamin Kwadjo Baah from Kumasi, and chased brass panels by Yekinni Folorunsho, from Oshogbo.

I also decided to focus on contemporary work from East and Southern Africa and compare it to the historical work of West Africa. To me, there is an obvious distinction between West and East Africa. In West Africa there is a continuity from the strong historical pieces, with older pieces still being used, festivals still involving some of these preserved pieces, new pieces still being commissioned, and blacksmiths continuing to make in these traditions. In East Africa, any contemporary blacksmith or metalworker has emerged not, perhaps, from a strong tradition, but from a domestic and economic necessity, often using recycled materials. With a very strong visitor and tourist market, it has been easier to adapt to making giftware to meet this market, than perhaps it would be in West Africa. In East Africa there is still a strong tradition of beadwork, and therefore adornment and jewellery were still likely to be areas of interest and artistic innovation.

Bracelet, Ian Auld Collection.

I found that the countries where this bead-work from stones and seeds was most apparent were Kenya and Tanzania, where workshops have been set up mainly by expatriate patronage, overseas art foundations and non-governmental organizations.

So the exhibition offers a chance to compare those two situations – where there is a very well-known, well-documented tradition of metalwork in West Africa, with the situation in East and Southern Africa, where metalwork seems to have emerged, as far as we know, much more recently?

There are older pieces from East Africa in museums, pieces from Karamoja in Uganda, some pieces from the Pokot and others from the Akamba, but these are mostly body adornment rather than large pieces. Similar pieces are still made and worn in rural areas. However, they are ethnic to the individual areas and groups.

When I was growing up at the coast in Kenya we used to have a lot of gold jewellery that was bought for us to mark various festivals. Over time, you built up your collection of gold bangles. But the market seems to have dried up, and the jewellery is now either Indian or Arabic, because it is cheaper to import, and is of the preferred very yellow gold. Although this is being bought and worn, it falls outside the scope of this exhibition. I was interested to discover who was buying the contemporary jewellery seen in crafts

shops, in cottage industry shops and charity initiatives.

I know that differences in training also interests you. In some areas most of the training is done by apprenticeship or learning by necessity and in others there has been the introduction of formal art schools and courses. Could you say more about this?

Most metalworkers have trained through the apprenticeship system. The brass casters in Benin in Nigeria, and Kumasi in Ghana, are trained in the context of the family. The traditional Asante apprentice-ship system has also survived in Kumasi. Male metalworkers, who make mainly jewellery, are commissioned to make pieces in the Asante tradition, by Asante men and women for their own use, particularly for their festivals and ceremonies. Examples of this work, depicting Asante iconography, are shown in the exhibition.

There is little or no institutional support for craft metalwork in Africa. Although there are a number of well established art colleges, the use of metal is restricted to sculpture. There are some notable exceptions, for example Kumasi's University of Science and Technology in Ghana, where there is a metalwork department in the art college, led by John Marmon Halm, whose work is included in the exhibition. There, jewellers and metalworkers are making pieces that are very international in

Necklace, African Heritage.

Overleaf: *Masqueraders,*
Yekinni Folorunsho.

outlook and approach. As John Marmon Halm's silver-plated tea and coffee set shows very well, they are not constrained by the traditional making of, say, the Lobi or the Asante, although they may include references to traditional designs.

Referring to other times and cultures in their work, as many artists and crafts people do in other parts of the world?

Yes. Also in northern Ghana, and in parts of Kenya, there are examples of traditional metalworkers including new images that they think will sell – the pieces can be very commercial – for example a ring might depict a modern chair, a police helmet, or a football hero.

But that's rather different to the college graduates reinterpreting old designs.

Yes, very different. These people have very little contact with the tools and materials available in art schools. They are working in a traditional art form, but are trying to adapt, to make their work innovative, so that the work can sell in the cities, where there is competition from those working in contemporary art.

That innovative approach, based on traditional training, is now more widespread. Among the metalworkers in Lagos in Nigeria, commissions to make very elaborate gates and railings for houses are extending the repertoire of the makers. The gates perform two functions –

they act as a deterrent to intruders and are looked upon as art pieces as well.

And who would commission such pieces?

Nigeria has a strong middle class and a number of wealthy people and for them such commissions show patronage for the arts, it also shows economic progress and acquirement.

Another type of producer is the one represented by the group in Oshogbo, also in Nigeria. Here, largely inspired by Nike Davies, co-founder of the Nike Centre for the Arts, young people have been encouraged to try sculptural metalwork. Many of the students are from rural areas. Nike Davies provides accommodation and tuition, and as the crafts people begin to sell their work, they are encouraged to set up their own studios. This sculptural work is beginning to find a market in Nigeria and has sold successfully in Germany and the USA. Yekinni Folorunsho works at the Centre.

I understand the textile makers at the Nike Centre also rely on the metalworkers' skills.

Yes, in the production of *adire* cloth, made by the Centre's textile co-operative, aluminium stencils with pictorial and geometric designs are used as templates for the application of the resist, before dying with indigo. Again these are included in the show.

36

people work, totally hitting the theory that in Africa people always need financial 'hand-outs'. For example, an enterprise zone in an area of Nairobi has been completely taken over by Jua Kali metal workers. There the competition is very fierce, with many stalls selling similar things. When you go to buy, you have a choice – do you choose by price or quality? Do you buy because the person is likeable or enterprising? Or do you buy for craftsmanship, or artistic quality? It gives the purchaser a chance to be extremely discerning; these craftspeople thrive within this critical environment.

And how wide a market do they have – do people travel far to buy from them?

People travel miles to the area, to buy their lamps, their domestic pots and pans – it is very large – it must cover at least two acres. Jua Kali themselves also travel, with their wares, to widen their market – rather like craftspeople in Britain travel to craft fairs.

Within this movement there are individuals, like Francis Kuaya Kiare. He makes individual pieces and has gained recognition, his work being commissioned by African Heritage, and through them, by others. His freedom of expression can be seen in the set of chairs with curved, painted backs, the candlesticks, and the humorous fireside tool-rack in the exhibition. His craftsmanship is in no doubt, nor is his individual style, even when he is making a series of limited editions.

In this way far more people are taking up an interest in metalwork as a way of exploring their art form. The East African equivalent is Jua Kali, set up in Kenya, by Kenyans. These innovative self-help schemes have been set up all over the country, in a wide range of crafts and industries.

Jua Kali simply means very hot – extreme heat. Anyone who is self-employed has to work hard, and they sweat a lot, and so they call themselves Jua Kali. Jua Kali has come to mean any self-initiated enterprise, motivated by the need to make a living. There is no charity involved, and no one has the means to raise a loan. People have found and created markets; they make what is widely needed. They have created employment, without multi-nationals, and without high investment – what they make has to sell. It was the most telling experience to see how hard these

Can you explain more about African Heritage?

African Heritage is part of the movement in Africa where art, craft and the giftware market exist hand in hand. Workshops are set up, unlike Jua Kali, by outside initiatives. The clientele also differs, and is basically among affluent tourists.

Are the tourists from outside Africa?

Yes, but slowly the indigenous people are starting to purchase some items. African Heritage is the fine end of the cottage industry. It was started by Joseph Murumbi, who was the first Kenyan Vice-President. He had travelled widely and had a collection of art from all over the world. He decided to start an art gallery, and employed Alan Donovan, an American painter, to set up the gallery with him. Later Alan became a partner. At first it sold African art – historical works and antiques – and then Alan, being a painter, became interested in contemporary work – painting and sculpture. He also became interested in African traditional fashion and jewellery. He started designing his own range, but based on traditional designs. You can see these influences in the exhibition – the traditional belt from the Akamba, and his own interpretation. His employees are apprenticed and trained by him.

In this exhibition I wanted to show that metalwork of quality is being made now, and that recycled metal does not only

generate toys; jewellery does not have to be only in gold or silver. And the design patterns that exist within the tradition can be extended; there need not be a stark distinction between traditional and contemporary, but a continuum. Within the traditions, there has been strong innovation – both the Maasai and Giriama in Kenya, for example, have been very innovative; now young makers need to be as innovative. I wanted us in Africa to look at what is our own, at the design possibilities that exist there, and to form it into a language that will be internationally recognized, but much more that we, as makers and users of this art, value our existing traditions. Any young person emerging from school today is not going to want to just copy and mimic traditional pieces, and why should they; we are not a static culture and neither are our ideas.

You don't want to reinforce a position which is out of date?

Exactly, unless it is necessary – as we found in Ghana among the Asante, where the festivals have continued to demand exact replication. Here, they still use traditional metalwork on ceremonial occasions and that continues to strengthen that tradition. But there is also room to buy other jewellery made in a very modern style – in most countries there is currently a fashion for wedding rings, a practice which came with the missionaries. I think that the merging of the two should exist – it exists in this country, where the Crown

Edan, Ian Auld Collection.

Jewels are still used, but not every day.
They co-exist alongside contemporary work.

You said that most of African Heritage work is bought by tourists. Is any made for export?

The intention of Joseph Murumbi and Alan Donovan was that the work should be bought by anybody

So, it is rather like the crafts in Britain?

This is the point I've been trying to make continually. I wanted to make a link and a comparison, between the structures that exist in Africa and those here.

There are Kenyan pieces in the exhibition which show the traditional work, pre-1950, and the modern work which grows out of it, both made of recycled metal.

So recycled materials have always been used?

Oh yes, the traditional piece was made by the Akamba people, for their own use, for their own festivals, like the Asante in Ghana. The new pieces derive from the tradition, but not necessarily for that tradition, but for any of us who wish to use them, so it is crossing the boundaries. These are designed by the Kenyan designer, Francis Kuaya Kiare, with Alan Donovan. They are made in his workshop, although some are commissioned from outworkers. Some of the pieces are taken directly from the traditional pieces.

Yes, the simple shape is good to wear and stands up wherever it is made.

Yes it does, and I think people in Britain making jewellery and metalwork are bound to be influenced by it because of its simplicity. When you visit art colleges it is simplicity that the students are looking for, and it is this interest which makes them look at African jewellery. In the exhibition they can see it at first hand, and can see what is being done in Africa now.

I have felt all along that the point of this exhibition wasn't to convince that the quality of African art exists — because everyone knows it does. I have tried to extend what is perceived as 'African' — to move on from 'the exotic, the ethnic' adornment and metalwork of the so-called 'disappearing tribes' to a fuller and more complete picture.

July 1995

Metalworking Techniques
Chris Russell

Mould in Furnace. Kaliijisa, Ghana.

Introduction

The principal metalworking operations are universal. However, throughout the world, metalworkers, whether as jewellers, smiths or casters, have taken processes and through an individual expression of skill imparted an essence that has associated processes with items and places in a unique manner.

All the processes examined here are part of the early development of metalworking technologies. Forging is the oldest metalworking skill, first employed to shape naturally occurring nuggets of non-ferrous metals. This is known as the lithic use of metals, which describes not so much the use of stones as hammers and anvils – stone anvils are still commonly used by rural blacksmiths in Africa – but the limited use of metals in keeping with other 'Stone Age' technologies. In comparison, the later discoveries of the metallurgical processes of smelting and casting released the true potential of ores.

Forging is not only a blacksmithing skill but it is also used by non-ferrous metalworkers as with the Akan, and goldsmiths in the Mopti and Djenne areas of southern Mali. One of the ultimate expressions of forged gold work, made for the Peul or Fulani women of southern Mali, has to be the four-lobed earrings each made from a solid gold billet. The Akan goldsmiths' principal use of hammered techniques is in the production of gold leaf. Here a billet of gold is repeatedly hammered to produce the thin gold leaf which is then used to cover carved wooden figures for linguist's staffs, bracelets and umbrella finials.

Lost-wax casting was being practised 2000 years before the discovery of iron working. In West Africa the practice includes the smaller solid castings such as the Akan goldweights and the majority of castings from the Savannah region, for example bracelets and anklets, although some of these anklets can weigh over a kilo.

Larger hollow castings are found in Nigeria, such as those from Tsoede and Ife, and direct castings of seeds and animal parts are documented from both the Akan and Savannah traditions of Ghana.

The smelting of copper ores in Africa, which had been confined to a few locations, has long been superseded by imported brass. The smelting of iron ores has, with a few exceptions, been carried out throughout the continent. But iron has also been imported in the form of bars or manillas since the beginning of the maritime trade with Europe and the majority of blacksmiths now utilize scrap iron and steels as their raw material. However, in remoter areas the practice of smelting has continued until recently as with the Busanga blacksmiths of south-east Burkina Faso and north-east Ghana.

Chasing is one of the decorative processes used to embellish either a flat or curved surface, or to give the finishing detail to cast or repoussé relief work. (The latter is where a relief is given to sheet metal by hammering it from the reverse side.) Chasing is sometimes referred to as punched decoration, as it utilizes small steel tools with the ends shaped to give impressions such as dots, lines or semi-circles. These are lightly held against the surface of the metal and tapped with a hammer to give the required detail and texture.

Forging

Forging is usually regarded as a blacksmithing skill, where the metal is heated and while still hot – when the material is soft – hammered into the required shape. When forging non-ferrous metals such as gold, silver and copper alloys, the metal is commonly worked cold. The inherent malleability of such metals, that is their property to be stretched and their thickness reduced, means that in the hands of a skilled craftsman a wealth of forms can be produced by careful hammering.

To produce the four-lobed earrings worn by the Peul women the goldsmith starts with a solid billet of gold, with the size relating to the intended size of the finished piece. The first stage is to hold the billet along the length of the edge of the anvil and direct the hammer blows to the edge of the billet. This produces a pinched indentation which is repeated on each side of the billet to produce a stunted cruciform section.

When the metal has been cold hammered it loses its malleability or becomes work-

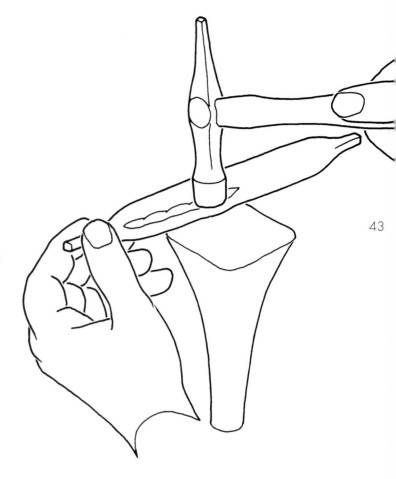

hardened. To restore the elasticity and prevent the metal cracking it needs to be annealed. Here the metal is slowly heated and allowed to cool. For silver and gold the temperature the metal needs to reach is between 600 and 650°C, when the metal starts to glow a dull red. The goldsmiths need to see this subtle change in colour and they work in a darkened environment. With its malleability restored the metal can continue to be forged.

Each of these short arms is again set on the anvil so that the metal can be further stretched and the distinctive lobes start to take their form. Each time the metal has been hammered it needs to be re-annealed. Gradually the metal is stretched both outward and along its length, at the same time thinning each lobe.

44

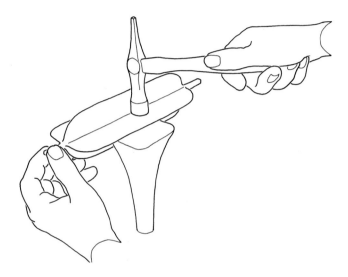

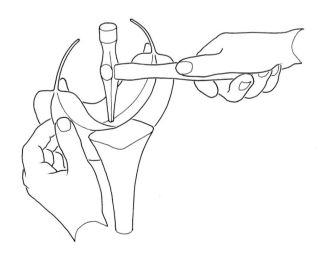

As well as ensuring that the rounded ends are formed the goldsmith also has to 'draw' two wires out of the centre which will be curved round to form the fastening.

Once the final length and shape have been achieved the lobes are then curved or twisted to complete the characteristic form. Again this is done through hammering. However, instead of holding the metal flat on the anvil so that it is stretched when hit with the hammer, it is held at an angle so that with each hammer blow the metal is slowly bowed to the required shape.

The major advantage of forging a piece of metal, especially gold or silver, is that there is minimal waste. A well-constructed piece will require no filing. (Files were only introduced into the Savannah and Sahel Regions during the colonial expansion from the end of the last century.) In addition a bright smooth hammer-face imparts its polish to the metal so reducing the amount of final polishing needed.

Smelting
There are few cases in Africa where metalworking is an exclusive occupation. It is invariably combined with farming, as seen with the Busanga blacksmiths. During the dry season, after the harvest has been collected, the blacksmiths will move away from the family compound searching for viable iron ore deposits. When a deposit is found a smelting furnace is built. Such furnaces are typically 1.25 m high and each furnace requires four bellows

which are individually made and operated in pairs by two smiths at a time.

The furnace is constructed using clay which is found in small deposits in shallow valleys. This is puddled with dried grass to give it strength. Balls of clay and grass are made and the furnace is built up as a series of rings to form a hollow column, tapering towards the top, with the structure appearing to lean backwards slightly. Two tuyères are constructed. These hollow conical forms direct the air into the heart of the furnace and are built into the bottom of the column. The four movable, pot-shaped bellows are also made, each having an integral air pipe, the tip of which rests inside the outer end of the tuyère. The goat skin which completes the bellow is then tied on to the 'pot' with a strip of rubber from a bicycle or car inner-tube. This is done in such a way as to form a flap. The smith holds the skin with his hand in the flap so that the circular pumping action on the upstroke allows the air into the bellow and on the down stroke closes the flap and pumps the air to the furnace. The smiths also collect wood from the area they are in and burn it in a hole dug into the ground to produce the necessary charcoal. The iron ore used is found as small irregular pebbles and is dug from shallow pits. These are hammered to break them into smaller pieces prior to being loaded into the furnace.

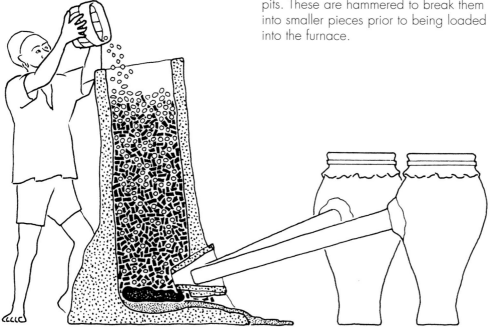

A day's smelting will start at first light. A fire is lit in the base of the furnace and charcoal is added to build up the fire. After this, charcoal and iron ore are added alternately into the top opening of the furnace.

The bellows are then positioned. After an hour of operating the bellows, the first quantity of slag needs to be tapped off. The slag, which collects at the very base of the furnace, is tapped out by breaking a small hole between the tuyères. After a further hour the furnace is recharged again with alternate layers of charcoal and ore. This pattern of tapping out the slag and re-charging the furnace can be repeated up to twelve times in a day, during which

time, if the clay shows signs of cracking, water is used to cool down the outside of the furnace and small repairs can be made.

The process continues for up to fourteen hours. Finally the bellows are lifted away and the furnace wall around the tuyères is hammered with an adze to break open the furnace. Wooden poles are placed in the tuyères to lift them away and the 'bloom' is then dragged out and water is used to quench the remaining charcoal so that it can be reused.

The bloom is an irregular shape, which has been likened to a solid sponge, and has inclusions of slag and charcoal. A bloom from such a smelting will produce about

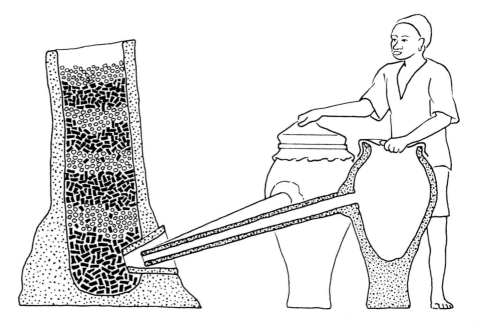

twelve hand-held hoe blades, but only after repeated hammering, first to eject the inclusions and then to produce a piece of metal of a standard thickness. This then can be cut into blanks from which each hoe blade is made.

The process of transforming a bloom into a useable form through heating and hammering, in a carbon-rich atmosphere, almost certainly produces a form of carbon steel. Such steels are capable of being hardened and tempered and thereby holding a sharpened edge. When hardened and tempered they are also considerably harder than mild steel, which constitutes the bulk of the scrap metal available – and are therefore less prone to wearing away when used on the hard lateritic soils that hoe blades have to till. Whether this process results in a true carbon steel with an even distribution of carbon through the material or is only case hardened – where there is a layer of carbon enriched iron at the surface – has yet to be fully demonstrated.

This process can be compared to the production of hoe blades by a group of Gurune smiths, from the upper east region of Ghana. They buy scrap iron railway sleepers from the modernization programme on Ghana's railways. These provide a raw material of a standard thickness which can be cut into seventy blanks each the same size, enabling over

thirty hoe blades to be made in a day.

While knowledge of the smelting of iron can still be found, it is unlikely to be retained by future generations as access to suitable scrap metals is the key to the success of rural blacksmiths such as these.

Lost-Wax Casting

Lost-wax casting allows the most intricate items to be cast by modelling the required form in beeswax. The model produced by casters is identical to the final object in every respect including its size and decorative detail. The nature of this process is such that no two castings are identical, as each wax model is 'lost' when the wax is melted out to leave the cavity in the mould. The mould is also destroyed when it is broken open, after the metal has been poured into it, so as to remove the casting.

The items being produced today by the Gurune casters from the upper east region of Ghana include the bracelet known as *banzire*, a larger version of which was made by previous generations of casters to be worn as an anklet. Casters model the wax in a quiet corner of their compounds. A hard wooden board is used to roll the wax on, which may be carved from a solid piece of wood with feet and handles. Various tools are also laid out. These may include a selection of wood and metal knives, modelling tools and formers used for moulding the wax and to give the circular form for bracelets. To make a

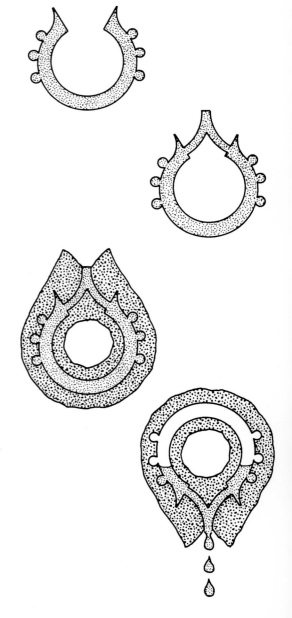

bracelet a wax 'sausage ' is rolled out which will form the centre of the wax model and have the decorative elements applied to it. The length of wax will be no more than 200 mm long and 8 mm in diameter. This length of wax is then formed into a circle with a small space between the ends. Finer wax 'wires' are then made by continuing to roll pieces of wax until they are about 1 mm in diameter. The wires are then placed onto the wax centre of the bracelet in a combination of straight lines and spiral strands. These strands are formed by twisting two fine wax wires together with a clockwise action before applying them to the wax centre. A further embellishment is to twist two wires with an anti-clockwise twist, which when laid alongside the former twisted strand, produces a herring-bone effect.

Banzire have two distinguishing features: two breaks in the decoration which are edged on either side by three small pellets, and thickened ends which can sometimes be slightly flared.

When the wax model is finished, a piece of wax is then rolled to make the runner. This is between 4 and 5 mm in diameter and folded to form a 'V'. This is attached to the end of the bracelet so that when it is cut off and filed the surface of the bracelet is not damaged.

The whole model is then totally encased in a mixture of clay and donkey dung, except for one place, the very end of the runner.

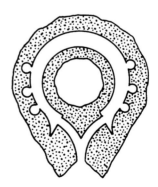

The mould is then heated up to melt the wax, which bubbles out of this hole. Some casters do this by precariously balancing the mould on the rim of the furnace. Others build a separate small fire from millet stalks. With the wax molten the mould is then held upside down over a bucket of water to collect the liquid wax for re-use.

Shallow clay crucibles are shaped to match the 'cup' of the mould, which is formed around the end of the runner to ensure that the molten metal is directed into the runners. The crucible is carefully stacked with the scrap metal from previous castings so as to get the greatest amount of metal into the crucibles. Brass from old bracelets is also used.

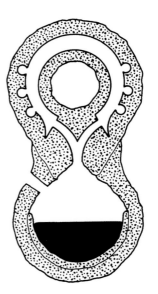

To complete the mould, it is then balanced on top of this mound of metal, and fresh pounded clay, including donkey dung, is plastered over the two parts to form one unit. A small hole is then made between the crucible and mould using a finger or a short stick. This vent allows the caster to see when the metal is molten and stops the mould exploding when heated. The moulds are finally covered in cold ash and left to dry out before being placed in the furnace.

It takes between one and a half and two hours to raise the temperature to the melting point of the metal, and the caster and an assistant will take turns to pump the single bellow. (Copper melts at 1083°C and most brasses melt between 950 and 1000°C.) During this time at least one

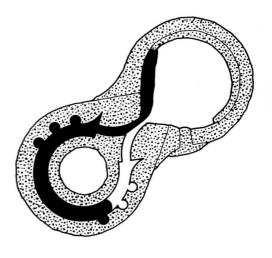

extra charge of wood and charcoal is
added to the furnace.

Just before the metal is ready to cast
patches of a bright yellow colour appear
on the moulds and a blue flame can be
seen from the air vent. Casters say they
can smell when the metal is molten. The
final check that the metal is ready to pour
is made by using an iron rod to poke into
the vent to see if the metal is liquid. Using
a pair of tongs the moulds are removed
from the furnace. The vent is plugged using
wet clay and the moulds are inverted and
set on the ground. They are then gently
rocked back and forth and tapped with the
back of a machete. This is to ensure that
no air is trapped in the mould which could
block the flow of metal and leave a gap
in the casting. The moulds are left to cool
slightly before the crucible section is cut
off. When the moulds have been
quenched they are broken open to reveal
the cast items. Although only partially
quenched and with the metal still hot, the
removal of the clay continues and, if
possible, the items are broken off the
sprues. The remaining sprues are chiselled
off with a machete and iron bar before
being stored. Finally they are filed to give
them a bright, if coarse, finish (often the
key selling feature) prior to taking them to
market.

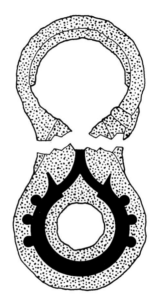

Chasing and Engraving

The surface of a metal object, whether flat or curved, can be embellished by engraving, chasing or repoussé work. Engraving involves the cutting of the surface with a hardened steel tool. Repoussé allows the creation of a relief from the underside of the piece of metal by hammering, which stretches the metal. Chasing on the top or upper surface uses small punches which are hit with a hammer to give detail or texture and a slight relief to the metal according to the shape of the punch, whether it be a dot, short line – similar to a cold chisel – a semi-circle or block of texture.

The Akan have used this technique on *kuduo* and *forowa* vessels made from copper alloys. The steel throwing-knives found through Central and Equatorial regions are engraved as are the Tuareg silver 'crosses'. In Ethiopia both engraving and chasing are used to embellish crosses, both processional and personal.

Metalworkers from Oshogbo in Nigeria have adopted the chasing technique for use on aluminium sheet. Aluminium is a softer metal than copper and commercially produced aluminium sheet is available in a variety of widths, and thicknesses of up to a millimetre.

As the material is too thin to be self-supporting it is placed on a wooden board to support the sheet whilst it is being worked on. The wood also absorbs the hammer blows and allows the aluminium sheet to respond to the impact of the chasing tools. The tools used are made by the chasers from scrap iron, each being individually shaped through forging and filing to produce the required mark on the metal that the chaser intends. While the softness of aluminium removes the need for the tools to be hardened and tempered, hardening and tempering will prolong the life of the tools, by reducing the need for reshaping and resharpening. Unlike gravers used on silver and steel, they should not be so sharp as to cut the thin aluminium sheet.

Yekinni Folorunsho, like all chasers from Oshogbo, does not set out his design in advance, but works directly on to the material using the chasing tools. Using themes from Yoruba mythology, the Bible and Islamic sources he traces the design using a short linear tool. He then gives volume and texture to the individual components, for example working on the figures before the trees and then the background texture.

The final piece may be a wall panel. This will need to be mounted on a wooden board or framed before being hung on the wall. Or smaller sections are produced to be fitted in door panels, which can complement the popular carved panels on doors found throughout the region.

Further Reading

54

The following list includes a selection of works devoted to the art of metalwork in Africa and a few others that will provide the interested reader with background information on African cultures. In addition, the Los Angeles-based quarterly journal *African Arts* regularly publishes articles on African metalworking traditions.

Ben-Amos, Paula Girshick, *The Art of Benin,* London: British Museum Press, 1995 (revised edition; first edition published 1980).

Brincard, Marie-Thérèse, *The Art of Metal in Africa,* New York: The African-American Institute, 1982 (exhibition catalogue).

Dewey, William J., and Allen F. Roberts, *Iron, Master of them All,* Iowa City: University of Iowa Museum of Art and the Project for Advanced Study of Art and Life in Africa, 1993 (exhibition catalogue).

Echoes of the Kalabari: Sculpture by Sokari Douglas Camp, Washington, DC: National Museum of African Art, Smithsonian Institution, 1989 (exhibition catalogue).

Fisher, Angela, *Africa Adorned,* London: Collins Harvill, 1987.

Garrard, Timothy F., *Akan Weights and the Gold Trade* (Legon History Series), London: Longman, 1980.

Garrard, Timothy F., *Gold of Africa: Jewellery and Ornaments from Ghana, Côte d'Ivoire, Mali and Senegal in the Collection of the Barbier-Mueller Museum,* Geneva: Barbier-Mueller Museum / Munich: Prestel, 1989.

Haaland, Randi, and Peter Shinnie (eds.), *African Iron Working: Ancient and Traditional,* Oslo: Norwegian University Press, 1985.

Herbert, Eugenia W., *Red Gold of Africa: Copper in Precolonial History and Culture,* Madison: University of Wisconsin Press, 1984.

Herbert, Eugenia W., *Iron, Gender, and Power: Rituals of Transformation in African Societies* (African Systems of Thought), Bloomington: Indiana University Press, 1993.

Herbert, Eugenia W., 'Africa, V. Materials, techniques and uses, 2. Metal', in Jane Shoaf Turner (ed.), *The Dictionary of Art,* London: Macmillan, forthcoming.

Lerer, Susan, *African Metalwork and Ivory,* Newport Beach, CA: Images of Culture, 1993 (exhibition catalogue).

McLeod, M.D. *The Asante,* London: British Museum Publications, 1981.

McNaughton, Patrick R., *The Mande Blacksmiths: Knowledge, Power, and Art in West Africa* (Traditional·Arts of Africa), Bloomington: Indiana University Press, 1988.

Plass, Margaret, *Seven Metals of Africa: Copper, Silver, Gold, Iron, Lead, Tin and Zinc,* Philadelphia: Philadelphia Museum of Art, 1959 (exhibition catalogue).

Willett, Frank, *African Art,* London: Thames and Hudson, 1993 (revised edition; first edition published 1971).

Acknowledgements

The Crafts Council is grateful to the following for their generosity in lending to this exhibition:

African Heritage, Nairobi; Patricia Arber; Ian Auld; Trustees of the British Museum; Stephen Goldsmith; Gordon Reece Gallery, Knaresborough; Juliet Highet; Horniman Museum and Gardens, London; Nellie Johansen; The Powell-Cotton Museum, Kent; Priscilla and Zbyszek Plocki; Chris Russell

Credits

Exhibition curator – Magdalene Odundo
Exhibition organisers – Conrad Bodman, Clare Cumberlidge, Ingrid Swenson
Exhibition designer – Barry Mazur
Exhibition graphics – Sally McIntosh

Photography
pages 6,10-11,13,14, 16-17, 20-21, 22, 40 Chris Russell
pages 24, 26, 31, 32, 34-35, 39 Sara Morris
pages 4, 8, 9,19, 28-29, 36 Nick Turner
Technical illustrations – Ted Hammond
Catalogue design – Pentagram
Printed by – Penshurst Press

Published in September 1995 to accompany the exhibition African Metalwork

Crafts Council Gallery
14 September to 19 November

Angel Row Gallery, Nottingham
2 December to 6 January 1996

© Crafts Council, 1995
ISBN 1 870145 52 6

44a Pentonville Road
Islington London N1 9BY
Telephone 0171 278 7700